JACKIE ROBINSON

Troll Associates

JACKIE ROBINSON

by Francene Sabin

Illustrated by Michael Sheean

Troll Associates

Library of Congress Cataloging in Publication Data

Sabin, Francene.
   Jackie Robinson.

   Summary: A biography of the black athlete who broke the
color barrier in major league baseball.
   1. Robinson, Jackie, 1919-1972—Juvenile literature.
2. Baseball players—United States—Biography—Juvenile
literature.   3. Segregation in sports—United States—
Juvenile literature.   4. Baseball—United States—History—
Juvenile literature.   [1. Robinson, Jackie. 1919-1972.
2. Baseball players.   3. Afro-Americans—Biography]
I. Sheean, Michael, ill.   II. Title.
GV865.R6S2   1985   796.357′092′4 [B] [92]   84-2603
ISBN 0-8167-0164-4 (lib. bdg.)
ISBN 0-8167-0165-2 (pbk.)

Baseball has long been considered America's national game. It is certainly an important part of American life. Sports fans root for their favorite teams and cheer for their favorite players. But until 1947, many fine athletes were barred from entering the major leagues—not because they weren't good enough, but because of the color of their skin.

Then, one gifted baseball player and remarkable human being smashed the barrier forever. His name was Jackie Robinson.

Jack Roosevelt Robinson, the first black man to play major-league baseball, was born on January 31, 1919, in Cairo, Georgia. He was the fifth child of Jerry and Mallie Robinson.

The Robinsons lived on a small farm where they were sharecroppers. That meant they rented the land on which they lived and paid the owner a large part of what they earned from farming the land. It was a harsh life.

When Jackie was only a few months old, his parents separated. Mrs. Robinson was left with five young children and no money to raise them. Her half brother, Burton McGriff, who lived in Pasadena, California, invited them to come and live with him. He said they could stay until they were able to afford a place of their own.

The Robinson family took the long train ride west and moved in with Uncle Burton. His apartment was just two rooms, but Mrs. Robinson was glad to have somewhere to stay. She quickly found work as a domestic servant in Pasadena. And as soon as she had saved enough money, she found a small house for herself and the family.

The Robinsons weren't much better off financially in California than they had been in Georgia. But they were better off in other ways. There was opportunity for black people to get a decent education in Pasadena. The same public schools were open to all children, while in Georgia the schools were segregated. This meant that black children in Georgia did not attend the same schools as white children. And Georgia's schools for black children were not as good as those attended by white children.

Yet even in unsegregated Pasadena, young Jackie encountered prejudice. He wasn't allowed to swim in the municipal pool with white children. He was hurt and confused by this and other prejudices.

Sometimes Jackie was angry and wanted to strike out at those who treated him unfairly. But he had a strong pride and will that stopped him from exploding. Even as a youngster he knew that if he fought every

time an injustice was done to him, he would
be spending the rest of his life fighting. Jackie
decided to answer back by using his skills as
an athlete and student.

Jackie had no father to guide him and teach him. But he did have an older brother. Mack Robinson was nine years older than Jackie. He was a good student and a great athlete. He could run faster and broad jump farther than anyone in California. In fact, Mack went on to win the silver medal in the 200-meter dash at the 1936 Olympic games.

Jackie wanted to be just like Mack. He attended the same schools—Cleveland Elementary School and Muir Technical High School. And at both, Jackie was the star athlete. At Muir High, he was the number-one player in baseball, football, basketball, and track. In addition, Jackie proved himself to be a very good student.

After graduating from Muir, Jackie entered Pasadena Junior College, where he set records in baseball and track and field. Then he transferred to the University of California at Los Angeles. There, he studied physical education with the hope of one day teaching it.

At the same time, Jackie was the star of UCLA's basketball, football, baseball, and track teams. He was the finest all-around athlete in the entire country.

Money problems forced Jackie to leave UCLA before he could graduate. He went to work as an athletic director for the National Youth Administration, a United States government agency, early in 1941.

That same year, he was asked to play in an all-star charity football game. This brought him to the attention of the Los Angeles Bulldogs, a professional team, which hired him to play for them. Jackie was with the Bulldogs until December 1941. Then America entered World War II, and Jackie enlisted in the army.

After completing Officer's Candidate School, Jackie was commissioned as a second lieutenant. But he didn't see combat because of a severe ankle injury. Instead, he spent his military service training troops for active duty. When he was honorably discharged from the army, Robinson took a job as athletic director of Samuel Houston College, a small school in Austin, Texas.

In the summer of 1945, Jackie played baseball with the Kansas City Monarchs, a team in the Negro American Baseball League. There were a number of fine players in the league, and he was one of the best. Yet even though the quality of baseball was excellent, the conditions were not.

Players in the Negro League were paid poorly, and they were discriminated against everywhere they went. They had to stay in run-down, segregated hotels, eat in second-rate cafes, and travel in segregated sections of buses and trains.

But the days of segregation in America were coming to an end. And one major-league baseball executive, Branch Rickey, decided to make it happen in his sport. His choice of the player to do it was Jackie Robinson.

Not only was Jackie an outstanding ball-player, he was an educated, thoughtful, self-controlled individual. He had to be all of those things to be able to take the abuse that was sure to greet his entrance into big-time baseball.

On October 23, 1945, Branch Rickey signed twenty-six-year-old Jackie Robinson to a contract with the Montreal Royals of the International League. The Montreal Royals were a minor-league team owned by the Brooklyn Dodgers, of which Mr. Rickey was president and general manager.

Robinson proved to be the perfect choice. In the 1946 season, as the Royals' second baseman, he led the league in batting average, number of hits, and number of runs scored. Robinson also led his team to the league championship.

Jackie was victorious in another way. No matter how much he was insulted and abused, he stayed cool and refused to be lured into a fight—on or off the playing field. When they had first met, Branch Rickey told Jackie Robinson, "I want somebody who has the guts not to fight back." Jackie was that man. He may have boiled inside, but he kept his anger under control. He let his superior talents answer his critics.

In the winter of 1947, Rickey invited Robinson to join the Dodgers at spring training camp. If he was good enough, and if he could continue to control his feelings, there would be a place for him on the major-league team.

Robinson came through admirably. On April 10, 1947, Rickey announced that Jackie Robinson would open the season with the Brooklyn Dodgers. Immediately, two Dodgers demanded to be traded to another team. They did not want to play with a black man.

This kind of outspoken prejudice and hate was leveled at Jackie from the opening game of the season. Robinson responded to this abuse as he had in the minor league, with quiet dignity and brilliant play.

In his rookie year as a Dodger, Jackie Robinson topped the league in stolen bases and enjoyed a fine all-around season at bat and in the field. His play helped the Dodgers win the National League pennant and won

him the Rookie of the Year award.

In the ten years that Jackie played for the Brooklyn Dodgers, he never gave less than his best. In that decade, the Dodgers won seven National League titles and one World Series. Jackie was voted the Most Valuable Player in 1949. That same year, he was the National League batting champion and led the league in stolen bases. He was truly a superstar and a favorite of fans everywhere.

When Robinson's baseball days ended, after the 1956 season, he took a job as vice president of a large chain of restaurants. He was responsible for maintaining good relations among the company's employees. The new position finally allowed Jackie to spend more time with his wife, Rachel, and their three children.

In 1962, Jack Roosevelt Robinson was elected to the Baseball Hall of Fame. He was the first black man to be honored in this way. It brought a moment of joy and satisfaction into his life at a time when he needed it, for Jackie was quite ill.

Jackie Robinson grew weaker and weaker. But he tried to remain active and was named a special assistant on community relations to the governor of New York. He was also a business executive and a supporter of the civil-rights movement. Then, on October 24, 1972—at the age of fifty-three—Jackie Roosevelt Robinson died.

His life had been a series of difficult challenges. And he had met each one with dignity and self control. Jackie Robinson is remembered not only because he was the first black man to break the color barrier in major-league baseball—but also because he was a truly remarkable human being.